THE ART OF PUBLIC SPEAKING

STUDENT CD-ROM GUIDEBOOK

McGraw-Hill College

*A Division of The **McGraw·Hill** Companies*

Student CD-ROM Guidebook Version 2.0 for
THE ART OF PUBLIC SPEAKING
Stephen E. Lucas

Published by McGraw-Hill, an imprint of The McGraw-Hill Companies, Inc. 1221 Avenue of the
Americas, New York, NY, 10020. Copyright © 2002 by Stephen E. Lucas. All rights reserved.
No part of this publication may be reproduced or distributed in any form or by any means, or stored
in a database or retrieval system, without the prior written consent of The McGraw-Hill Companies,
Inc., including, but not limited to, in any network or other electronic storage or transmission, or
broadcast for distance learning. Some ancillaries, including electronic and print components,
may not be available to customers outside the United States.

1 2 3 4 5 6 7 8 9 0 CSS/CSS 0 9 8 7 6 5 4 3 2 1

ISBN 0-07-250121-9

www.mhhe.com

THE ART OF PUBLIC SPEAKING

STUDENT CD-ROM GUIDEBOOK

*A clear, concise explanation of how to use the tools
found on the CD-ROM.*

Boston   Burr Ridge, IL   Dubuque, IA   Madison, WI   New York   San Francisco   St. Louis
Bangkok   Bogotá   Caracas   Kuala Lumpur   Lisbon   London   Madrid   Mexico City
Milan   Montreal   New Delhi   Santiago   Seoul   Singapore   Sydney   Taipei   Toronto

Bridging the Printed Page

CONTENTS

and the Spoken Word

GETTING STARTED

WINDOWS	MACINTOSH
1. Insert Disk 1: The Art of Public Speaking Student CD-ROM 2.0 into the CD-ROM drive.	1. Insert Disk 1: The Art of Public Speaking Student CD-ROM 2.0 into the CD-ROM drive.
2. Click on the Start button on your Desktop and select Run.	2. Double-click on the CD-ROM icon, which will say Public Speaking.
3. Type D:\ (or the letter of your CD-ROM drive). Click OK.	3. Double-click on start.html.
4. Double-click start.html.	

Following these instructions for Windows and Macintosh will launch your browser and you can begin using the program. If your browser does not launch, see the readme.txt file on the CD-ROM for more information.

Installing Internet Explorer and QuickTime

The software includes separate programs for installing Internet Explorer and QuickTime on Windows and Macintosh systems. See the readme.txt file on the CD-ROM for more detailed information.

For Technical Support, Call Toll-Free 1-800-331-5094

BASIC FEATURES

Fully integrated with the textbook, this CD-ROM has been created to help you master the principles discussed in the book and apply them in your speeches.

CD-ROM icons in the margin of the book will guide you to corresponding features on the CD.

View the discussion of practicality in Renee Varghese, "Multicultural, Multilingual."

CD: Video Clip 15.1

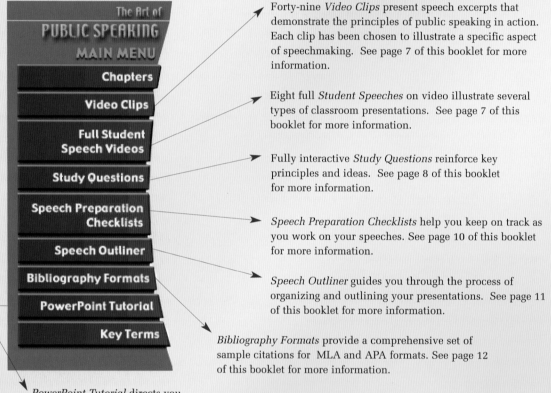

Forty-nine *Video Clips* present speech excerpts that demonstrate the principles of public speaking in action. Each clip has been chosen to illustrate a specific aspect of speechmaking. See page 7 of this booklet for more information.

Eight full *Student Speeches* on video illustrate several types of classroom presentations. See page 7 of this booklet for more information.

Fully interactive *Study Questions* reinforce key principles and ideas. See page 8 of this booklet for more information.

Speech Preparation Checklists help you keep on track as you work on your speeches. See page 10 of this booklet for more information.

Speech Outliner guides you through the process of organizing and outlining your presentations. See page 11 of this booklet for more information.

Bibliography Formats provide a comprehensive set of sample citations for MLA and APA formats. See page 12 of this booklet for more information.

PowerPoint Tutorial directs you through the basics of using PowerPoint as a presentation aid. See page 13 of this booklet for more information.

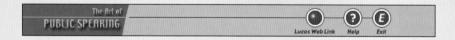

The Lucas Web Link provides instant access to a wide range of resources for the public speaking course. See page 9 in this booklet for more information.

For Technical Support, Call Toll-Free 1-800-331-5094

and the Spoken Word

VIDEOS

Clips (Disk One)

Forty-nine Video Clips present speech excerpts that demonstrate the principles of public speaking in action. Each clip has been chosen to illustrate a specific aspect of speechmaking. Two-thirds of the clips are from classroom presentations; the others are from well-known public figures.

Chapter 1   **1-1** The Power of Public Speaking (Famous Speakers)

Chapter 2   **2-1** Maintaining Free Speech (Edward Kennedy) **2-2** Maintaining Free Speech (Colin Powell)

Chapter 4   **4-1** Choosing a Speech Topic **4-2** Phrasing a Central Idea

Chapter 5   **5-1** Adapting to the Audience (Barbara Bush) **5-2** Capturing the Attention of the Audience **5-3** Adapting to Audience Attitudes **5-4** Using Audience-Analysis Questionnaires

Chapter 7   **7-1** Using Hypothetical Examples **7-2** Using Examples to Reinforce Ideas **7-3** Using Statistics to Support Ideas **7-4** Making Statistics Meaningful to the Audience **7-5** Identifying the Source of Speech Testimony

Chapter 8   **8-1** Using Transitions **8-2** Combining Internal Summaries and Transitions **8-3** Using Signposts

Chapter 9   **9-1** and **9-2** Relating to the Audience in a Speech Introduction **9-3** Using a Story in a Speech Introduction **9-4** Presenting Preview Statements **9-5** Using a Crescendo Ending (Martin Luther King) **9-6** Linking the Conclusion to the Introduction

Chapter 11   **11-1** Creating Imagery (Ronald Reagan) **11-2** Exploiting the Rhythm of Language (Winston Churchill) **11-3** Using Imagery and Rhythm

Chapter 12   **12-1** Speaking from a Manuscript (Ann Richards) **12-2** Speaking Extemporaneously (Elizabeth Dole) **12-3** Using Vocal Variety **12-4** Using Gestures and Eye Contact

Chapter 13   **13-1** Presenting Visual Aids (Norman Schwarzkopf) **13-2** Using a Model as a Visual Aid **13-3** Using Videotape as a Visual Aid **13-4** Demonstrating a Procedure **13-5** Explaining Visual Aids to the Audience

Chapter 14   **14-1** Relating to the Audience in Speaking to Inform **14-2** Avoiding Technical Language in Speaking to Inform **14-3** Personalizing Ideas in Speaking to Inform

Chapter 15   **15-1** Demonstrating Practicality in Speaking to Persuade **15-2** Using Problem-Cause-Solution Order **15-3** Using Monroe's Motivated Sequence

Chapter 16   **16-1** Establishing Credibility **16-2** Using Emotional Appeal (Mary Fisher)

Chapter 17   **17-1** Speaking to Commemorate (Ronald Reagan) **17-2** Using Humor (Barbara Bush)

Appendix A   **A-1** Presenting the Introductory Speech **A-2** Presenting the Introductory Speech **A-3** Presenting the Introductory Speech **A-4** Presenting the Introductory Speech

Full Student Speeches (Disk Two)

Eight full Student Speeches provide real examples of several types of presentations.

1 A Mile in My Shoes (Introductory with Visual Aid) 2 Kiyomi and Me (Introductory) 3 A Family Tradition (Introductory) 4 Questions of Culture (Commemorative) 5 Cryonics (Informative) 6 Dying to Be Thin (Informative) 7 Self-Defense on Campus (Persuasive) 8 The Ultimate Gift (Persuasive)

For Technical Support, Call Toll-Free 1-800-331-5094

Bridging the Printed Page

STUDY QUESTIONS

To help you test your understanding of key principles and ideas, the CD-ROM 2.0 contains a comprehensive set of study questions for each chapter. These questions are interactive and systematically cover all the major concepts discussed in the book.

Study questions use a variety of formats

- Multiple-choice
- True-false
- Fill-in
- Essay
- Sentence-select

After you enter your answer for each question, you will receive not just an indication of whether the answer is right or wrong, but feedback that explains the correct answer.

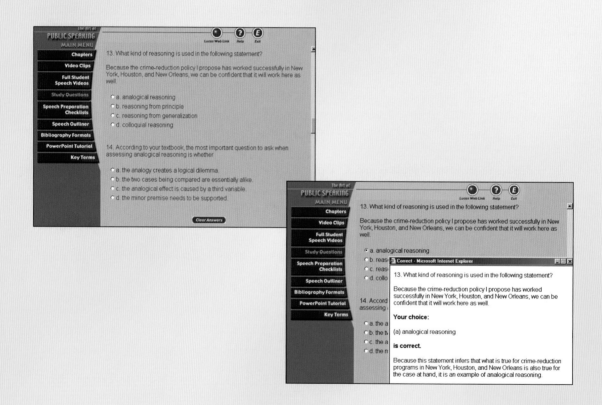

and the Spoken Word

LUCAS WEB LINK

While using The Art of Public Speaking CD-ROM 2.0 you can connect to the Lucas website where you will find more tools for studying and speech preparation.

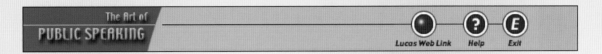

Many students have told us that they study for exams by focusing on key terms. The Flashcards and Crossword Puzzles use the glossary from the textbook to create interactive formats for studying terminology. There is one Crossword Puzzle and one set of Flashcards for each chapter of the book.

Glossary Flashcard   Glossary Crossword Puzzle

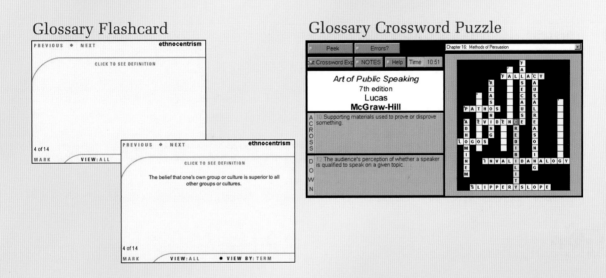

The Lucas website provides other study tools for each chapter—including learning objectives, chapter outlines, chapter summaries, and practice quizzes.

Top 100 Speeches of the 20th Century

Compiled by Stephen E. Lucas and Martin J. Medhurst, this list of the 20th century's best American speeches reflects the opinions of 137 scholars of public address. In addition to listing the top 100 speeches, the Lucas website provides a link to the text of each speech.

For Technical Support, Call Toll-Free 1-800-331-5094

SPEECH PREPARATION CHECKLISTS

There are 12 Speech Preparation Checklists to help you keep on track as you prepare your speeches. These checklists are fully coordinated with the textbook and cover all the major elements of speech preparation.

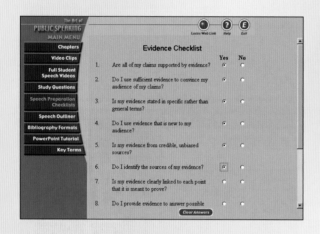

- Ethical Public Speaking Checklist

- Specific Purpose Checklist

- Central Idea Checklist

- Supporting Materials Checklist

- Main Points Checklist

- Speech Introduction Checklist

- Speech Conclusion Checklist

- Preparation Outline Checklist

- Checklist for Preparing Visual Aids

- Checklist for Presenting Visual Aids

- Evidence Checklist

- Reflective-Thinking Method Checklist

SPEECH OUTLINER

This software guides you through the process of organizing and outlining your presentations.

As you use the outliner, you will move step by step through each element of your speech beginning with the title and ending with the bibliography. Help screens explain the organizational methods involved in outlining each part of the speech.

When you get to the body of your speech, the outliner automatically formats your points in accordance with proper outlining principles.

The outliner also allows you to save, revise, and print your work — as well as export it to your own word processor.

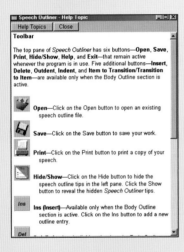 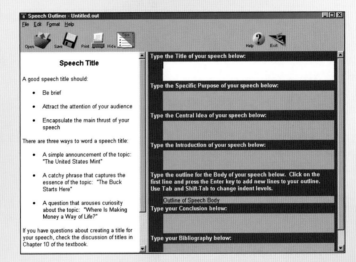

For Technical Support, Call Toll-Free 1-800-331-5094

BIBLIOGRAPHY FORMATS

Bibliography Formats provide sample APA and MLA citations for all major types of source material, including

Books

Newspapers

Magazines

Scholarly journals

Government publications

Reference works

Personal interviews

Television programs

Internet documents

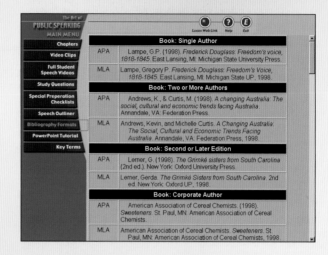

KEY TERMS

Throughout the book, key terms are defined in the margin as they appear in the text. Those key terms are reproduced on the CD-ROM, where they can be accessed either by chapter or by a master glossary arranged in alphabetical order. Whether you are reviewing for exams or working on a speech, you can instantly check the meaning of any key term with the click of a mouse.

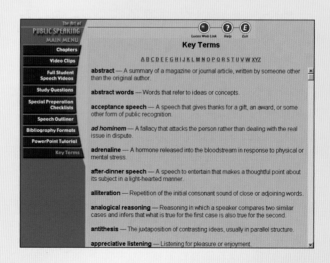

For Technical Support, Call Toll-Free 1-800-331-5094

and the Spoken Word

POWERPOINT TUTORIAL

The PowerPoint Tutorial is a quick guide to using PowerPoint as a presentation aid for speeches. The Tutorial reviews basic principles such as:

Using Color

Choosing Fonts

Adding Clip Art

Giving Your Presentation

Full PowerPoint Tutorial Contents

For Technical Support, Call Toll-Free 1-800-331-5094

USING THE ART OF PUBLIC SPEAKING CD-ROM 2.0 OUTSIDE THE CLASSROOM

Whether preparing for a speech or studying for an exam, students spend a good amount of time working on their own—outside of class at a time that is right for their schedules.

Most of the resources on The Art of Public Speaking CD-ROM were designed with this reality in mind.

These resources include 49 video clips of public speakers in action that illustrate various aspects of the speechmaking process (details on page 7 of this booklet), eight full student speeches that exemplify different types of classroom presentations (details on page 7), speech preparation checklists (details on page 10), an interactive speech outliner (details on page 11), study questions (details on page 8), a glossary of all key terms from the book (details on page 12), and a PowerPoint Tutorial (details on page 13).

Read through this booklet to discover the range and volume of resources offered by the CD-ROM—even in the middle of the night.

For Technical Support, Call Toll-Free 1-800-331-5094

USING THE ART OF PUBLIC SPEAKING CD-ROM 2.0 TO HELP WITH SPEECH ANXIETY

Practically every tool on The Art of Public Speaking CD-ROM was designed to help overcome the fear of speaking in public by becoming more knowledgeable about and comfortable with the process of preparing and delivering a speech.

➤ Study Questions and Key Terms help you master principles and concepts discussed in the book. Video clips and full sample speeches help take the mystery out of speechmaking so you can feel more confident making your own presentations.

➤ Speech Preparation Checklists, Speech Outliner, Bibliography Formats, and PowerPoint Tutorial help you with every aspect of speech preparation from selecting a specific purpose through creating an outline and using visual aids.

It's no wonder that students who tested the CD-ROM in a recent study described it as a great confidence builder.

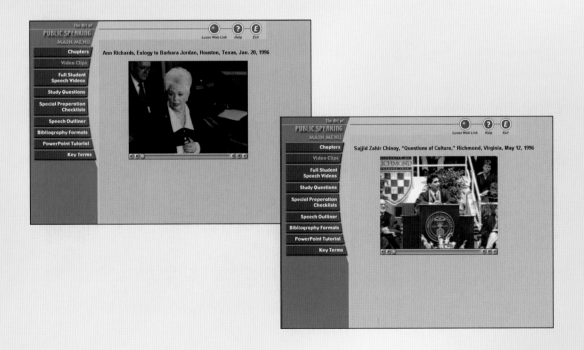

For Technical Support, Call Toll-Free 1-800-331-5094

USING THE CD-ROM 2.0 TO IMPROVE SPEECH DELIVERY

When it comes to speech delivery, there is no substitute for experience and practice. Yet students have told us that they also profit enormously from seeing videos of other speakers in action.

Disk One of The Art of Public Speaking CD-ROM 2.0 contains 49 video clips that demonstrate the principles of effective speech delivery discussed in the textbook. Two-thirds of these clips are from student presentations; the rest are from public figures such as Martin Luther King, John F. Kennedy, Colin Powell, and Elizabeth Dole. In addition to illustrating effective delivery skills, these clips provide an opportunity to experience some of the most important public speeches of recent years.

Disk Two of the CD-ROM includes eight complete student speeches. Three of these are introductory speeches that help with the daunting task of delivering your first classroom presentation. There are also two persuasive speeches, two informative speeches, and one commemorative speech. Seven of the speeches on Disk Two are printed in the book, so you can read the speeches and then see how they come across when presented orally.

If you are using visual aids in your speech, the Visual Aids Checklist can help you with this aspect of speech delivery. If you are using PowerPoint, you can turn to the PowerPoint Tutorial for assistance.

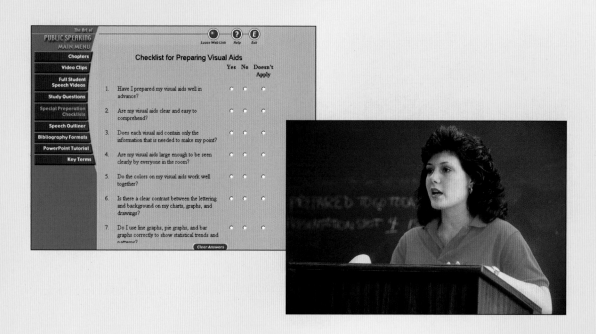

For Technical Support, Call Toll-Free 1-800-331-5094

and the Spoken Word

Using the CD-ROM 2.0 to Organize and Outline a Speech

Learning how to organize one's ideas for effective communication is one of the most important skills learned in a public speaking class. Like the textbook, The Art of Public Speaking CD-ROM was created to help you with this vital skill.

The Speech Outliner is a powerful program that takes you step by step through the process of organizing and outlining a speech. Help screens explain the organizational methods used in each part of the speech, and the outliner automatically formats the body of the speech in accordance with proper outlining principles. The outliner also allows you to save, revise, and print your work, as well as to export it to your own word processor.

If you need a bibliography with your outline, the Bibliography Formats can help ensure that your citations are entered correctly.

As you work on organizing your speeches, you can also turn to the Main Points Checklist, the Speech Introduction Checklist, the Speech Conclusion Checklist, and the Preparation Outline Checklist—all of which are included on the CD-ROM. These checklists make it easier to apply the principles of speech organization discussed in the book.

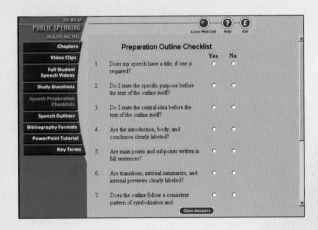

For Technical Support, Call Toll-Free 1-800-331-5094

USING THE CD-ROM 2.0 TO DEVELOP CRITICAL-THINKING SKILLS

One of the most important parts of public speaking is thinking. As you work on constructing your speeches with accuracy, order, and clarity, you are also engaged in the process of thinking with accuracy, order, and clarity. Like the textbook, The Art of Public Speaking Student CD-ROM is designed to enhance your skills of critical thinking as well as your skills of speech delivery.

In addition to helping you prepare for exams, the CD's Study Questions encourage you to think critically about concepts discussed in the book.

Because so much of critical thinking depends on the ability to organize one's ideas clearly and effectively, the Speech Outliner is much more than a technical guide to creating outlines—it can also help build your critical-thinking skills.

Several of the Speech Preparation Checklists contribute to critical thinking, including the Checklist for Ethical Speaking, the Specific Purpose Checklist, the Central Idea Checklist, the Supporting Materials Checklist, the Main Points Checklist, the Evidence Checklist, and the Reflective-Thinking Checklist.

Thinking critically also means citing the sources of one's ideas. The Bibliography Formats on the CD-ROM help you do this by providing examples of MLA and APA citation formats for two dozen kinds of source material—from books, essays, and newspaper articles to government publications, personal interviews, television programs, and Internet documents.

For Technical Support, Call Toll-Free 1-800-331-5094

USING THE CD-ROM 2.0 TO PREPARE FOR TESTS

There are several tools on The Art of Public Speaking CD-ROM that can help you prepare for tests. By using the Study Questions, you can check your knowledge of each chapter in the book. These study questions are fully interactive. After you enter your answer for each question, you will receive an indication of whether the answer is correct or incorrect, plus feedback that explains the correct answer. The Study Questions cover all the major concepts in the book and come in a variety of formats (multiple-choice, true-false, fill-in, essay, and sentence-select).

Some students have told us that they prefer to study for examinations by focusing on key terms from the book. The CD-ROM provides a complete glossary of key terms and definitions. You can also connect to the Lucas website and study terminology by using the Flashcards and Crossword Puzzles found there. These two features make studying key terms more interesting than simply reading words and their definitions. There is one Crossword Puzzle and one set of Flashcards for each chapter of the book.

Use this booklet for more information on Study Questions (page 8), the Lucas Web Link (page 9), and Flashcards and Crossword Puzzles (page 9).

Study Question

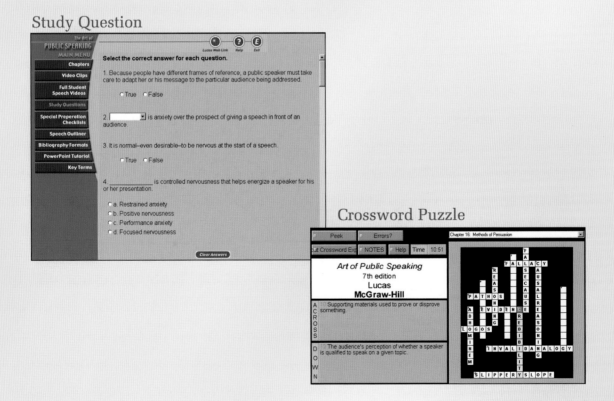

Crossword Puzzle

For Technical Support, Call Toll-Free 1-800-331-5094

TECHNICAL SUPPORT

1-800-331-5094

If you have any questions or experience any difficulties using this software program, please call our toll-free service line Monday-Friday from 8 AM to 4:30 PM Central Standard Time.

MINIMUM SYSTEM REQUIREMENTS

WINDOWS

* Windows 95, 98, or NT 4.0
* 24MB RAM (32MB recommended)
* Pentium II or faster
* CD-ROM drive 4x or faster
* sVGA color monitor running at least 256 colors and a resolution of 800 x 600
* SoundBlaster or compatible sound card
* External speakers or headphones
* Netscape Navigator 4.5 (or higher) or Internet Explorer 5.0 (or higher)
* QuickTime 4.0

MACINTOSH

* Operating system 7.5, 8.0 or 8.5
* 24MB RAM (32MB recommended)
* Power PC Processor or faster
* CD-ROM drive 4x or faster
* Color monitor running at least 256 colors and a resolution of 800 x 600
* External speakers or headphones
* Netscape Navigator 4.5 (or higher) or Internet Explorer 4.5 (or higher)
* QuickTime 4.0

For Technical Support, Call Toll-Free 1-800-331-5094